BAVARIA

TRAVEL GUIDE 2024-2025

Your Essential Companion to Discovering Scenic Trails, Legendary Castles, Historical Landmarks and Authentic German Cuisine.

Cedric J. Stone

COPYRIGHT

All rights reserved. No part of this publication may be reproduced, distributed, or transmitted in any form or by any means, including photocopying, recording, or other electronic or mechanical methods, without the prior written permission of the publisher, except in the case of brief quotations embodied in critical reviews and certain other non-commercial uses permitted by copyright law.

Copyright © 2024 by Cedric J. Stone

TABLE OF CONTENTS

Gratitude..7
    Welcome to Bavaria...11
    Geographical Overview.. 11
    Cultural Insights... 13
    Why Visit Bavaria in 2024-2025?...15
    How to Use This Guide... 17

CHAPTER ONE... 19
    Practical Information..19
    Travel Essentials..20
    Currency and Banking..20
    Language and Communication..21
    Weather and Best Time to Visit.. 22
    Getting There...24
    Navigating Bavaria...27
    Health and Safety... 28
    Customs and Etiquette.. 29
    Tipping...30

CHAPTER TWO.. 31
    Accommodations... 31
    Luxury Hotels... 32
    Mid-range Hotels in Bavaria... 39
    Budget-Friendly Stays in Bavaria.......................................45

Unique Accommodations...51

Booking Tips... 55

CHAPTER THREE...57

Dining and Cuisine.. 57

Introduction to Bavarian Cuisine...58

Influence of Beer in Bavarian Cuisine...63

Beer Gardens and Halls...64

Restaurant Recommendations... 65

Traditional Bavarian Cuisine... 66

Modern Bavarian Dining...68

Street Food and Casual Dining.. 70

Dinner Etiquette in Bavaria...72

Culinary Events and Festivals.. 73

CHAPTER FOUR... 77

Top Attractions and Activities in Bavaria....................................77

The Bavarian Alps..78

Munich: The Bavarian Capital...79

Nuremberg: A Medieval Gem... 84

Regensburg: A UNESCO World Heritage Site............................ 88

Bamberg: The City of Seven Hills... 91

Berchtesgaden.. 94

The Romantic Road.. 97

Bavarian Festivals and Cultural Events............................... 100

CHAPTER FIVE... 103

Sample Itineraries.. 103
Three-Day Highlights Tour... 104
One-Week Cultural Exploration... 106
Family-Friendly Adventures... 109
Outdoor and Nature Lovers' Itinerary....................................... 110

CHAPTER SIX... **113**

Shopping and Entertainment.. 113
Shopping in Bavaria... 114
Nuremberg: Traditional Crafts and Markets............................. 116
Regensburg: Historical Shopping Streets................................. 117
Ingolstadt Village: Outlet Shopping... 118
Bamberg: Antiques and Local Specialties................................ 119
Entertainment in Bavaria.. 120
Classical Music and Opera... 121
Theater and Performing Arts.. 123
Nightlife and Modern Entertainment... 125

CHAPTER SEVEN.. **127**

Outdoor and Adventure Activities... 127
Hiking and Walking Trails... 128
Skiing and Snowboarding... 130
Cycling and Mountain Biking.. 133
Water Sports.. 135
Climbing and Mountaineering... 138
Paragliding and Hang Gliding... 140

CHAPTER EIGHT **143**
    Local Insights and Tips 143
    Understanding Bavarian Culture 144
    Practical Travel Tips 145
    Responsible Travel 147

CHAPTER NINE **151**
    Resources and Contacts 151
    Tourist Information Centers 152
    Emergency Contacts 154
    Helpful Apps and Websites 156
    Consulates and Embassies 159

BONUS SECTION **163**
    Hidden Gems in Bavaria 163
    Basic Vocabularies In German 174

Gratitude

Dear Readers,

Thank you for choosing this book to guide you on your next adventure. Your interest and curiosity are greatly appreciated, and I am grateful for the chance to share the beauties of our world with you. Before you begin the adventures detailed within these pages, I'd like to express my heartfelt gratitude.

Your support means everything to me, and I am confident that this book will be a valuable companion on your journey. Whether you're planning your first vacation or returning to uncover new treasures, you'll find inspiration, practical insights, and a greater bond with the places you visit.

Enjoy every second of your journey, and may your memories be as breathtaking as the sights you will see.

Thank you for your participation in our adventure.

BAVARIA, GERMANY MAP

HOW TO SCAN THE QR CODE

1. Open your smartphone's camera or QR code scanner app.
2. Point the camera at the QR code.
3. Wait for the camera to recognize the code.
4. Tap the notification or link that appears.
5. Follow the link or instructions provided.

INTRODUCTION

Welcome to Bavaria

Bavaria, Germany's largest federal state, is a land of enchanted beauty, rich history, and thriving culture. Located in the country's southeastern portion, Bavaria is a fusion of gorgeous landscapes, including towering Alps, undulating hills, and vast forests. With its alluring blend of tradition and modernity, Bavaria provides visitors with an experience unlike any other, complete with attractive towns, stately castles, and a deep-rooted cultural heritage that continues to thrive.

Geographical Overview

Bavaria is the largest of Germany's sixteen states, covering over 70,550 square kilometers in total. Its diverse terrain includes the spectacular Bavarian Alps in the south, where peaks like the Zugspitze, Germany's highest peak, climb into the sky. The alpine terrain is ideal for outdoor enthusiasts, with chances for skiing, hiking, and mountaineering. To the north, the landscape transitions into the Franconian Jura and Bavarian Forest, which are recognized for their lush woodlands and tranquil beauty.

The state is surrounded by Austria and the Czech Republic, and its proximity to both nations lends a distinct cross-cultural character. Bavaria's major rivers, including the Danube, Main, and Inn, serve as lifelines for trade and pleasure, adding to the state's beautiful charm.

Historical Context

Bavaria has a millennium-long history, beginning as a powerful duchy in the early Middle Ages. It became a kingdom in 1806, and the many opulent palaces and castles dotting the landscape reflect its regal history. The most well-known of these is

Neuschwanstein Castle, a fairytale building erected by King Ludwig II that attracts millions of visitors each year.

Throughout history, Bavaria has had a profound impact on Germany's political and cultural scene. The region was a power center during the Holy Roman Empire and later became a German Renaissance hotspot. Bavaria's rich past is maintained in its numerous museums, historic places, and traditions, which are still cherished today.

Cultural Insights

Bavaria is known for its distinct culture, which includes its language, festivals, and customs. The Bavarian dialect, a variety of German, is widely spoken and regarded as a source of regional pride. Bavarians are renowned for their generosity and warmth, greeting visitors with open arms and a hearty "Grüß Gott" (God bless you).

The Oktoberfest, the world's largest beer festival held annually in Munich, is one of Bavaria's most well-known cultural exports. This renowned event draws millions of tourists from all over the world, eager to join in the festivities, which feature traditional Bavarian music, food, and, of course, beer. Oktoberfest celebrates Bavarian culture and highlights the region's gastronomic delights, including pretzels, sausages, and roast pork.

Bavarian culture is deeply rooted in Catholic traditions, as evidenced by the numerous religious festivals and activities occurring throughout the year. These include the attractive Christmas markets that illuminate towns and cities over the holiday season, selling homemade items, mulled wine, and festive happiness.

Why Visit Bavaria in 2024-2025?

Bavaria, a region rich in history, culture, and breathtaking landscapes, is a must-visit destination in 2024-2025. Whether you're seeking picturesque villages, world-class museums, or outdoor adventures, Bavaria has it all. Its iconic blend of medieval charm and modern vitality offers an unforgettable travel experience.

First, Bavaria's stunning landscapes are a nature lover's dream. From the snow-capped Alps to the rolling hills of the Franconian countryside, you can hike, ski, or simply marvel at the scenic beauty. Neuschwanstein Castle, perched dramatically on a hilltop, looks like a fairytale come to life and is a must-see for history enthusiasts and photographers alike.

The region's cities are equally captivating. Munich, Bavaria's capital, is famous for its lively beer gardens, the grand Marienplatz square, and the annual Oktoberfest, the largest beer festival in the world. But there's much more to Bavaria than beer. Nuremberg offers a deep dive into Germany's history, with its well-preserved medieval architecture and significant WWII sites.

In 2024-2025, several special events will make a visit to Bavaria even more enticing. Cultural festivals, Christmas markets, and seasonal events celebrate the region's rich traditions. Bavarian cuisine, from hearty sausages to soft pretzels and sweet strudels, will delight food lovers.

Finally, Bavaria's welcoming atmosphere, efficient public transport, and diverse accommodation options make it an easy and rewarding destination for all types of travelers. Whether you're exploring quaint villages or bustling cities, Bavaria in 2024-2025 promises an adventure filled with beauty, history, and charm.

How to Use This Guide

Welcome to the "Bavaria Travel Guide 2024-2025"! This book has been designed to be your ultimate companion while exploring Bavaria, whether you're planning your trip or already on the go. To make the most of this guide, here's how you can navigate through it:

Start by diving into the "Introduction" section, where you'll get a feel for Bavaria's geography, culture, and traditions. This section sets the stage for understanding the region and its rich history before you embark on your adventure.

Next, head over to the "Practical Information" section in "Chapter One". This chapter provides all the essentials you need to prepare for your trip, including currency, banking, language tips, and guidance on the best times to visit. Use the transportation tips to ensure smooth travel, and brush up on customs and etiquette to feel confident in local interactions.

"Accommodations" in "Chapter Two" offers a range of lodging options, from luxury hotels to unique Bavarian stays. Whether you're a budget traveler or seeking indulgence, you'll find recommendations tailored to your style.

For foodies, "Dining and Cuisine" section in "Chapter Three" will guide you through Bavarian culinary delights. From traditional dishes to modern dining experiences, this section ensures you savor every bite of your journey.

Explore the "Top Attractions" section in "Chapter Four" for must-see spots, or flip to the "Sample Itineraries" section in "Chapter Five" for pre-planned routes based on your interests.

Use the "Shopping and Entertainment" section and the "Outdoor and Adventure" chapters to fill your days with fun, whether you prefer browsing local markets or hitting the hiking trails.

Keep the "Resources and Contacts" section handy for useful information throughout your trip. Enjoy Bavaria!

CHAPTER ONE

Practical Information

Bavaria, with its rich history and dynamic culture, is a captivating destination for travelers. Before embarking on your journey to this wonderful region, it is essential to be well-prepared with practical information that will enhance your experience and ensure a smooth and enjoyable vacation. This chapter offers a comprehensive reference to the practical aspects of vacationing in Bavaria, covering everything from travel necessities to transit options.

Travel Essentials

Visa Requirements

Bavaria is a part of Germany, which is a Schengen Area member. Travelers from the Schengen Zone do not require a visa for short stays of up to 90 days. Visitors from non-Schengen nations, such as the United States, Canada, Australia, and Japan, can also enter Germany without a visa for up to 90 days for tourism or business. However, travelers from other countries may need a Schengen visa, which can be obtained via the German consulate or embassy in their home country.

It's important to note that visa requirements sometimes vary, so check the latest restrictions on the official German Federal Foreign Office website or contact your local German consulate before visiting.

Currency and Banking

The Euro (€) is the official currency in Bavaria and throughout Germany. ATMs are widely available around the region, enabling simple access to cash.

Most major credit and debit cards are accepted in hotels, restaurants, and shops, but it's a good idea to carry cash for smaller establishments or remote areas where card payments may be unavailable.

When using ATMs, keep in mind that foreign transaction fees and exchange rates may apply. It is also essential to notify your bank of your vacation plans in order to avoid any problems with card usage while overseas.

Language and Communication

Bavaria's official language is German, and while many locals speak English, particularly in tourist areas, it is helpful to know some basic German phrases. Bavarians frequently speak a distinct regional dialect, but standard German is well understood.

Here are some helpful German phrases to get you started:

- Hallo - Hello.
- Auf Wiedersehen - Goodbye.

- Bitte - Please.
- Danke - Thank you.
- Ja - Yes.
- Nein - No.
- Entschuldigung - Excuse me.
- Do you speak English? - Sprechen Sie Englisch?

A translation tool or phrasebook might also be handy for more complicated conversations.

Weather and Best Time to Visit

Bavaria has a continental climate with different seasons, each providing unique chances for exploration and activities:

Spring (March – May)

Spring is a wonderful time to visit Bavaria because the countryside bursts with colorful blooms and lush foliage. Temperatures gradually rise, ranging from 5°C (41°F) to 20°C (68°F), making it ideal for outdoor activities such as exploring gardens and parks. Popular activities during this season include the Frühlingsfest (Spring Festival) in Munich, which offers a taste of Bavarian culture and food.

Summer (June-August)

Summer is Bavaria's busiest tourism season, with average temperatures ranging from 18°C (64°F) to 25°C (77°F). The beautiful weather is ideal for hiking in the Alps, visiting outdoor beer gardens, and attending festivals like the Tollwood Summer Festival in Munich. However, it is also the busiest time of year, so early reservations for accommodations and attractions are advised.

Autumn (September–November)

Autumn in Bavaria is distinguished by warm weather and breathtaking fall scenery. Temperatures range from 10°C (50°F) to 18°C (64°F), providing a magnificent setting for exploring the countryside and attending Oktoberfest, the world's most famous beer festival held in Munich. This season is great for learning about Bavarian culture and sampling the region's delectable cuisine.

Winter (December - February)

Winter transforms Bavaria into a magical wonderland, with temperatures ranging from -5°C (23°F) to 5°C (41°F). The Alps provide superb skiing and snowboarding options, while Christmas markets fill towns and cities with festive spirit. Winter sports fans and those looking for a cozy, authentic Bavarian experience will have much to enjoy this season.

Getting There

Bavaria has an efficient and well-connected transportation network, making it easy for visitors to explore the region. The following are the available means of transportation available in Bavaria:

By Air:

Munich International Airport (MUC) is the major entrance to Bavaria and one of Germany's busiest airports. It operates various international and domestic flights that connect Bavaria to important cities across the world. Nuremberg Airport (NUE) is another option for travelers, offering more connections, notably inside Europe.

By Train:

Germany's extensive rail network, run by Deutsche Bahn (DB), enables easy access to Bavaria from surrounding nations. High-speed trains, such as the

ICE (Intercity-Express) and EuroCity, connect Munich, Nuremberg, and other Bavarian cities to important European cities such as Vienna, Zurich, and Prague.

By Car:

For those traveling by automobile, Bavaria is accessible via Germany's autobahn network. The A9, A3, and A8 highways are important arteries connecting Bavaria to other parts of Germany and abroad. Car rentals are accessible at major airports and cities, allowing you to explore the region at your own pace.

Navigating Bavaria

Public Transportation

Bavaria's public transportation system is efficient and dependable, with buses, trams, and trains to help you get around cities and towns. Munich's MVV network is substantial, featuring U-Bahn (subway), S-Bahn (suburban rail), buses, and trams. Nuremberg and other cities have similar systems, making it easier to travel around without a car.

Regional Trains

Regional trains operated by DB Regio and other local operators provide a handy way to travel between cities and rural areas. The Bavaria Ticket provides unrestricted travel on regional trains, buses, and trams within Bavaria for one day, providing outstanding value for visiting several destinations.

Cycling and Walking

Bavaria is a bike-friendly region with several cycling routes and clearly signposted paths. Many cities offer bike-sharing programs, and cycling is a fantastic way to explore both metropolitan areas and the scenic countryside. Walking is also an excellent way to see Bavarian towns and cities, with pedestrian-friendly streets and scenic routes.

Health and Safety

Bavaria is a safe and welcoming destination, but it's always a good idea to plan ahead of time to ensure a trouble-free trip. The following are core aspects of this facet:

Health Care

Germany offers a high standard of healthcare, and travelers can find great medical facilities throughout Bavaria. EU nationals can use their European Health Insurance Card (EHIC) to access healthcare services, however visitors from other countries are advised to have medical travel insurance.

Pharmacies (Apotheken) are extensively available, providing both over-the-counter drugs and prescription services. Many pharmacies have extended hours, and emergency services are available 24/7.

Customs and Etiquette

Understanding local customs and etiquette can improve your stay in Bavaria and enhance positive interactions with its people. The following should be kept in mind as regards customs and etiquette in Bavaria:

Greetings and Social Norms

- **Greetings:** Bavarians often greet with a firm handshake and maintain eye contact. A polite "Grüß Gott" or "Hallo" is a standard greeting.

- **Punctuality:** Being on time is vital in Bavarian culture, so plan to arrive promptly for appointments and social events.

- **Dinner Etiquette:** When dining in Bavaria, wait to be seated and keep your hands visible on the table. It is customary to say "Guten

Appetit" before beginning a meal, and "Prost" when clinking glasses.

Tipping

Tipping is customary in Bavaria, and it is typical to round up the amount or add an extra 5-10% for excellent service. In restaurants, tip the server directly rather than leaving it on the table.

Being well-prepared with practical information is critical to having a memorable and enjoyable stay in Bavaria. From visa requirements and transportation alternatives to local customs and safe travel practices, this chapter equips you with the information you need to make the most of your trip through this captivating region. As you explore Bavaria's diverse landscapes and dynamic culture, you'll discover a destination that offers the ideal balance of tradition and modernity, welcoming you with open arms to make unforgettable memories.

CHAPTER TWO

Accommodations

Finding the appropriate location to stay is an important aspect of any trip experience, and Bavaria has a variety of accommodations to suit every taste and budget. From luxurious hotels and beautiful boutique inns to low-cost hostels and one-of-a-kind stays in castles or alpine huts, Bavaria offers a variety of lodging options that reflect the region's rich history and diverse terrain.

This chapter explores the various types of accommodations accessible, providing insights into what distinguishes each option and how to select the best fit for your trip.

Luxury Hotels

Bavaria, with its stunning landscapes and rich cultural legacy, boasts some of Germany's most elegant and renowned hotels. These establishments provide unmatched service, exquisite amenities, and one-of-a-kind experiences that capture the region's beauty and refinement. Whether you're seeking a tranquil retreat in the Alps :or a lavish stay in the center of Munich, Bavaria's luxury hotels cater to the most discerning guests. Here are five popular luxury hotels in Bavaria, each providing a unique experience:

Hotel Bayerischer Hof, Munich

Why Stay Here?

Hotel Bayerischer Hof is one of Bavaria's most prominent hotels, situated in the heart of the city. It has approximately 340 luxurious rooms and suites, each beautifully designed in a mix of traditional and contemporary designs. The hotel has a rooftop spa with panoramic views of the city, five restaurants serving a variety of cuisines, and six bars, including the famous Falk's Bar, which is set in a medieval hall.

The hotel also has a nightclub, a theater, and a large meeting and event area, making it an ideal destination for both pleasure and business travelers. Its central location allows easy access to Munich's greatest attractions, including Marienplatz and Viktualienmarkt.

Price Range: The average price range is around €350 to €6,000 per night, depending on the room or suite type.

Schloss Elmau Luxury Spa Retreat and Cultural Hideaway

Why Stay Here?

Schloss Elmau, located in the Bavarian Alps, is a one-of-a-kind retreat that combines elegance and serenity. The hotel offers two distinct retreats: a premium spa retreat and a cultural refuge. It has world-class spa amenities, including multiple pools, saunas, and treatment rooms, as well as yoga and exercise programs.

Schloss Elmau is also renowned for its cultural activities, which include concerts and literary events in its concert hall. Guests can enjoy fine dining in the hotel's multiple restaurants, which specializes in gourmet food made with organic and locally sourced ingredients. The neighboring mountain beauty makes an excellent backdrop for outdoor activities such as hiking and skiing.

Price Range: The average price range is around €600 to €2,500 per night, depending on the room or suite class.

Mandarin Oriental, Munich

Why Stay Here?

The Mandarin Oriental in Munich is a luxurious hotel on a quiet street near the city's famous

Maximilianstrasse. The hotel's 73 spacious rooms and suites combine elegant European style with subtle Asian influences. Guests can enjoy the rooftop pool and patio, which provide spectacular views of the Munich skyline.

Dining options include Matsuhisa Munich, and the Lounge, well-known for its afternoon tea. The hotel's central position makes it ideal for discovering Munich's cultural attractions and luxury shopping.

Price Range: The average price range is around €900 to €4,000 per night, depending on the room or suite class.

Hotel Vier Jahreszeiten Kempinski, Munich

Why Stay Here?

The Vier Jahreszeiten Kempinski, located on the prominent Maximilianstrasse, is a historic hotel renowned for its luxurious and superb service. It has 305 spacious rooms and suites with attractive interiors, a spa with a pool and fitness center, and many dining options, including the Schwarzreiter Tagesbar & Restaurant, which offers contemporary Bavarian cuisine.

The hotel's location allows guests convenient access to Munich's cultural attractions and luxury shopping. Its stately lobby, known as the "Jahreszeiten Lobby," is a favorite spot to drink coffee and eat pastries.

Price Range: The average price range is around €550 to €3,500 per night, depending on the room or suite class.

Kempinski Hotel, Berchtesgaden

Why Stay Here?

The Kempinski Hotel Berchtesgaden, located in the magnificent Bavarian Alps, provides a spectacular mountain retreat. The hotel has spacious rooms and suites with alpine views, a luxurious spa, and a variety of eating options, including Restaurant Le Ciel, which serves gourmet food. Outdoor enthusiasts can go skiing, hiking, and golfing in the neighboring area.

Price Range: The average price range is around €350 to €1,500 per night, depending on season and accommodation type.

These luxury hotels in Bavaria and its surroundings offer a blend of opulence, comfort, and unique experiences, making them ideal for discerning tourists looking for exceptional accommodations.

Mid-range Hotels in Bavaria

Mid-range hotels in Bavaria offer a comfortable and affordable stay by combining modern amenities with traditional Bavarian charm. Here are five popular mid-range hotels that provide exceptional value and their distinctive features:

Hotel Torbräu, Bavaria, Munich

Why Stay Here?

Hotel Torbräu, located in the center of Munich, offers an ideal balance of tradition and modern luxury. This family-run hotel is conveniently located near Marienplatz, making it an ideal base for exploring Munich's attractions. The hotel features elegantly designed rooms with modern amenities including free Wi-Fi, flat-screen TVs, and air conditioning.

Guests can enjoy a complimentary breakfast buffet, and the on-site restaurant, Schapeau, serves both Bavarian and foreign cuisine. The hotel's friendly staff and central location make it a popular choice among guests seeking convenience and comfort.

Price Range: The average price range is around €150 to €200 per night.

Hotel Eisenhut, Rothenburg

Why Stay Here?

Hotel Eisenhut, located in the old town of Rothenburg, combines traditional beauty with modern amenities. The hotel, housed in a collection of 16th-century houses, offers attractively designed rooms with ancient antiques and modern amenities.
Guests can dine in the on-site restaurant, which serves traditional Franconian cuisine and has breathtaking views of the Tauber Valley. The hotel's central location gives guests convenient access to Rothenburg's historic sights and cobblestone streets.

Price Range: The average price range is around €120 and €180 per night.

Hotel Goliath am Dom, Regensburg

Why Stay Here?

Hotel Goliath am Dom, located in Regensburg, a UNESCO World Heritage city, provides a combination of sophistication and comfort. The hotel features modern rooms with elegant decor, free Wi-Fi, and minibars.

Guests can begin their day with a wonderful breakfast buffet and relax in the on-site sauna. Its exceptional position, only steps from Regensburg Cathedral and the Stone Bridge, makes it an ideal base for visiting the city's cultural attractions.

Price Range: The average price range is around €130 to €200 per night.

Hotel Victoria, Nuremberg

Why Stay Here?

Hotel Victoria is a lovely, independently-run hotel in the center of Nuremberg's Old Town. The hotel's rooms are distinctively decorated and equipped with modern amenities such as flat-screen TVs and complimentary WiFi. Guests can enjoy a hearty breakfast buffet in the airy breakfast area before relaxing at the hotel's bar and terrace. The hotel's proximity to sights such as Nuremberg Castle and the German National Museum makes it an excellent base for cultural exploration.

Price Range: The average price range is around €110 to €160 per night.

Hotel Metropol, Munich

Why Stay Here?

Hotel Metropol, located just a few minutes' walk from Munich's central train station, provides a convenient and comfortable stay in the city center. The hotel's rooms are modern and well-appointed, with amenities like free Wi-Fi, flat-screen TVs, and soundproof windows to ensure a restful night's sleep. Guests can enjoy a complimentary breakfast buffet with a selection of Bavarian specialties. The hotel's central position makes it ideal for visiting Munich's attractions, such as Marienplatz and the Englischer Garten.

Price Range: The average price range is around €100 to €150 per night.

These mid-range hotels strike a balance between comfort, convenience, and affordability, making them ideal for tourists wishing to enjoy Bavaria's diverse landscapes and rich cultural heritage.

Budget-Friendly Stays in Bavaria

Bavaria has several lodgings that offer exceptional value without sacrificing comfort or enjoyment. Here are five popular, budget-friendly lodgings in Bavaria, highlighted by their qualities and price ranges:

Wombat's City Hostel, Munich

Why Stay Here?

Wombat's City Hostel is a popular choice among budget tourists due to its dynamic atmosphere and handy location near Munich's central train station. The hostel provides a variety of lodging options, including both dormitory-style and private rooms.

Guests can relax in a large community room with a bar, lounge, and kitchen facilities. The hostel also offers free Wi-Fi, a laundry facility, and 24-hour reception. Social activities and guided city tours are often scheduled, making it simple for guests to meet other tourists.

Price Range: Rooms range from €50 to €80 per night, while private rooms go for approximately €80 per night.

Euro Youth Hotel, Munich

Why Stay Here?

Euro Youth Hotel, located around Munich's central train station, offers a budget-friendly historic structure with a cozy environment. The hostel has a bar with daily happy hours, a lounge room, and a shared kitchen. Rooms vary from shared dormitories to private en-suite alternatives. The friendly staff gives free city maps and travel assistance, and the hotel's proximity to public transportation allows you to easily explore the city.

Price Range: Rooms go for €50 per night, with private rooms available from €70.

Jugendherberge Nuremberg

Why Stay Here?

This youth hostel, located within the ancient Kaiserburg Castle in Nuremberg, provides a unique and economical stay with panoramic views of the city. The hostel mixes modern conveniences with historical charm, offering dormitory-style and private family rooms. Guests can enjoy a complimentary breakfast buffet, on-site dining options, and guided city tours. The hostel's location also provides convenient access to Nuremberg's Old Town and key attractions.

Price Range: Rooms range from €50 to €60 per night, while private rooms are available from €70.

Pension Vötterl, Bad Reichenhall

Why Stay Here?

Pension Vötterl, located in the charming town of Bad Reichenhall, offers a low-cost refuge with breathtaking views of the surrounding mountains. The guesthouse offers basic, comfortable accommodations and a regular breakfast buffet. Guests can unwind in the garden or explore neighboring hiking and biking paths. The pension is ideally situated for trips to Salzburg, Berchtesgaden, and Königssee.

Price Range: Rooms are available from €50 per night.

Hotel Pension Schmellergarten, Munich

Why Stay Here?

Hotel-Pension Schmellergarten is a comfortable and reasonably priced guest house in Munich's Ludwigsvorstadt area, close to public transit and popular attractions such as the Theresienwiese and Marienplatz. The guesthouse offers basic, comfortable rooms with en suite or communal bathrooms. Every morning, guests can enjoy a delicious breakfast, free Wi-Fi, and courteous service. Its welcoming atmosphere and convenient location make it a popular choice among budget travelers.

Price Range: Single rooms go for around €60 per night, with double rooms available at approximately €80 per night.

These budget-friendly stays in Bavaria provide exceptional value for money, with pleasant accommodations and easy access to the region's attractions without breaking the bank.

Unique Accommodations

Castle Stays

Staying at a Bavarian castle is a magical experience that allows guests to step back in time, immersing them in history and grandeur. The following are examples of popular castles in Bavaria:

Schloss Kronberg

Why Stay Here?

Located in Kronberg im Taurus, this fairy-tale castle features elegant rooms, fine dining, and wonderfully landscaped gardens. Guests can enjoy sports such as horseback riding and golf on the estate's grounds.

Hotel Burg Colmberg

Why Stay Here?

Situated within a historical medieval castle in Colmberg, this hotel overlooks the gorgeous Franconian landscape and combines ancient elegance with modern comfort. Guests can explore the historic edifice, eat gourmet cuisine, and admire panoramic views from the castle's towers.

Alpine Huts and Mountain Lodges

Staying in an alpine hut or mountain lodge provides a rustic and exciting experience. These lodgings allow you to disconnect from the contemporary world and experience Bavaria's natural splendor. The following are some of Bavaria's popular alpine huts and mountain lodges:

Höllentalangerhütte, Garmisch-Partenkirchen

Why Stay Here?

Nestled in the breathtaking Höllental Valley, this mountain hut offers basic accommodation for hikers and climbers. It serves as a starting point for ascents to Germany's highest peak, the Zugspitze.

Berghotel Rehlegg, Ramsau

Why Stay Here?

Located in the Berchtesgaden Land district, this eco-friendly mountain lodge offers comfortable rooms with stunning views of the Bavarian Alps. Guests can enjoy hiking, spa treatments, and local food in a tranquil mountain location.

Booking Tips

When reserving accommodations in Bavaria, consider the following recommendations to ensure a smooth and enjoyable stay:

- **Plan Ahead:** Bavaria is a popular location, particularly during peak tourist seasons. Book your accommodations in advance to secure your preferred choice and benefit from early booking discounts.

- **Compare Options:** Use internet travel sites to compare costs, read reviews, and look into alternative lodging options. Websites such as Booking.com, Airbnb, and TripAdvisor offer helpful insights from other travelers.

- **Flexible Dates:** If your trip dates are flexible, consider traveling during the mid seasons (spring and autumn), when accommodations are less expensive and attractions are less crowded.

- **Check Inclusions:** To ensure you're receiving good value for your money, consider what's included in the accommodation price, such as breakfast, Wi-Fi, parking, and access to facilities.

- **Special Requests:** If you have any unique needs or preferences, such as accessibility or dietary restrictions, contact the accommodation ahead of time to make adjustments.

Bavaria has a vast choice of lodgings to suit all preferences and budgets, ensuring that every traveler can find the ideal location to stay. Whether you seek luxury in a stately hotel, charm in a boutique inn, or adventure in a mountain lodge, Bavaria's hospitality ensures an unforgettable stay. You can enhance your vacation through this wonderful region by selecting the best accommodations based on your interests and travel style. As you visit Bavaria's cultural riches and stunning landscapes, finding the proper location to rest your head will be an important part of your Bavarian experience.

CHAPTER THREE

Dining and Cuisine

Bavaria's rich culinary legacy tantalizes the senses, with a broad range of flavors reflecting deep-rooted traditions and cultural influences. From hearty entrees to exquisite desserts, Bavarian cuisine celebrates local ingredients and traditional recipes. This chapter delves into Bavaria's dining culture, showcasing must-try dishes, the influence of beer, and a guide to the best of Bavarian food and dining.

Introduction to Bavarian Cuisine

Bavarian cuisine is known for its heartiness and simplicity, characterized by substantial quantities and rich tastes. The region's culinary traditions are influenced by its agricultural terrain, with a focus on locally supplied meats, dairy, and cereals. Bavarian cuisine is heavily impacted by its historical and cultural ties with neighboring regions, resulting in a distinct blend of German, Austrian, and Bohemian flavors.

Must-Try Dishes:

The following are some of the most popular and exquisite Bavarian cuisine:

Weisswurst

Weisswurst is a typical Bavarian sausage composed of minced veal and pork back bacon, seasoned with fresh herbs and spices. It is often served in a bowl of hot water and eaten in the morning, with freshly baked pretzels and sweet mustard. Traditionally, Weisswurst is eaten without the casing, which is peeled off before consumption. This meal is a Bavarian breakfast favorite and pairs well with a refreshing wheat beer.

Schweinshaxe

Schweinshaxe (pork knuckle), a traditional Bavarian meal, is a savory pleasure. The pig knuckle is slowly roasted until the skin is crispy and the meat is soft. It is frequently served with sauerkraut, red cabbage, and potato dumplings (knödel). This meaty dish is a popular choice at beer halls and festivals, providing a true flavor of Bavarian culture.

Leberkäse

Leberkäse is a Bavarian meatloaf made with finely ground corned beef, pork, and bacon, which is baked to a crispy crust. It is commonly sliced and served warm with mustard and bread rolls, making it a popular snack or lunch option. Leberkäse is commonly available at street food booths and butcher shops across Bavaria.

Brezen (pretzel)

Bavarian pretzels, or "Brezen", are an iconic representation of the region's culinary tradition. These huge, soft pretzels have a golden-brown shell and a soft interior seasoned with coarse salt. Brezen is a popular dinner addition, commonly served with beer and Weisswurst or as a standalone snack.

Obatzda

Obatzda is a creamy cheese spread made with Camembert or Brie, butter, and spices like paprika and caraway seeds. It is traditionally served with freshly made pretzels and is a popular meal in Bavarian beer gardens. Obatzda's rich, savory flavor pairs well with a cool beer.

Kaiserschmarrn

Kaiserschmarrn is a typical Bavarian delicacy that resembles shredded pancakes. The batter is formed from eggs, flour, sugar, and milk, which is then fried in butter and caramelized before being torn into pieces. It is usually sprinkled with powdered sugar and served with fruit compote or apple sauce. This delicious dessert is popular among both locals and visitors.

Influence of Beer in Bavarian Cuisine

Bavaria is identified with beer, and its brewing traditions are an important element of the region's culture and food. The Reinheitsgebot, or German Beer Purity Law, was established in Bavaria in 1516 to ensure the quality and purity of beer produced. Bavaria is home to some of the world's oldest breweries, and beer is frequently considered a mainstay of Bavarian cuisine.

Beer Varieties

Bavaria has a wide range of beer varieties, each with its own flavor character and brewing process:

- **Helles:** A pale lager with a smooth, mild flavor, Helles is a popular choice in Munich beer halls.

- **Dunkel:** A dark lager with a deep, malty flavor, Dunkel is popular during the colder months.

- **Weissibier:** Also known as wheat beer, Weissibier is distinguished by its hazy appearance and fruity, yeasty aroma.

- **Bock:** A robust, full-bodied beer traditionally brewed for festivals and special events.

Beer Gardens and Halls

Beer gardens (Biergärten) and beer halls (Bierhallen) are fundamental to Bavarian social life, providing a welcoming environment for both locals and visitors to enjoy traditional cuisine and drink. These establishments frequently provide classic Bavarian meals alongside a selection of beers, resulting in a lively dining experience. The following are some of the most popular beer halls in Bavaria:

Hofbräuhaus

Hofbräuhaus, one of the world's most well-known beer halls, provides an authentic Bavarian experience with its lively atmosphere, traditional music, and hearty cuisine.

Augustiner Braustuben

This beer hall is a Munich local favorite, known for its historical charm and outstanding beer.

Restaurant Recommendations

Bavaria's culinary landscape provides a diverse range of dining alternatives, from historic Bavarian taverns to modern restaurants providing inventive food. Here are some recommended traditional Bavarian dining establishments to visit:

Traditional Bavarian Cuisine

Zum Franziskaner, Munich

Why Dine Here?

Located in the heart of Munich, close to the Bavarian State Opera, this is a historic restaurant that serves classic Bavarian meals in a traditional atmosphere. Zum Franziskaner, well-known for its Weisswurst and Schweinshaxe, provides an authentic Bavarian experience.

Price Range: The average price range for meals is between €3 and €35.

Schlenkerla, Bamberg

Why Dine Here?

Located in the historic town of Bamberg, this restaurant offers a unique dining experience with its smoked beer and Franconian delicacies.

Price Range: The average price range for meals is between €5 and €15.

Modern Bavarian Dining

Bavaria offers an array of modern cuisine. Here are some recommended contemporary dining establishments to visit:

Tantris, Munich

Why Dine Here?

Tantris is a michelin-starred restaurant that offers a modern take on Bavarian cuisine with a focus on fresh, locally sourced ingredients. It is well-known for its innovative cuisine and sophisticated dining atmosphere.

Price Range: The average price range of meals is between €130 and €300.

EssZimmer, Munich

Why Dine Here?

Located in BMW Welt, EssZimmer combines Bavarian cuisine with foreign influences in a stylish setting. The restaurant provides a gourmet dining experience centered on seasonal ingredients.

Price Range: The average price range for dinners is between €120 and €300.

Street Food and Casual Dining

Bavaria offers an array of street food and casual dining. Here are some recommended casual dining establishments to visit:

Viktualienmarkt, Munich

Why Dine Here?

Viktualienmarkt, a lively food market in the heart of Munich, features a diverse selection of street food stalls and casual cafes. Visitors can try Bavarian specialties such as Leberkäse, Brezen, and Obatzda.

Wurstkuchl, Regensburg

Why Dine Here?

Wurstkucht is a traditional sausage kitchen near the Stone Bridge in Regensburg that serves grilled sausages and handmade mustard. It is a must-see for visitors looking for authentic Bavarian street food.

Dinner Etiquette in Bavaria

Understanding Bavarian dining etiquette can improve your food experience and promote nice interactions with locals. The following are core values of Bavarian etiquette:

Table Manners

- **Greetings:** When you enter a restaurant, greet the personnel with a cheerful "Grüß Gott" or "Guten Tag."

- **Seating:** In casual dining establishments, particularly beer gardens, it is common to seat yourself unless otherwise ordered by the staff.

- **Toasting:** When toasting, make eye contact and say "Prost" before taking a sip of your beverage.

- **Pace of Dining:** Bavarian dining is often slow, with an emphasis on enjoying the meal and company. Take your time and relish every course.

Culinary Events and Festivals

Throughout the year, Bavaria conducts a variety of culinary events and festivals to celebrate its rich food and beverage traditions. The follow are some of its most common culinary events and festivals:

Oktoberfest

Oktoberfest, the world's largest beer festival, takes place every year in Munich and draws millions of tourists from all over the world. The festival incorporates traditional Bavarian music, food, and beer, resulting in a lively and festive atmosphere. Visitors can taste traditional foods like Schweinshaxe, Brezen, and Obatzda while taking in the lively festivities.

Nürnberger Christkindlesmarkt

The Nürnberger Christkindlesmarkt is one of Germany's oldest and most well-known Christmas markets, hosted in Nuremberg. The market sells a variety of holiday goodies, such as gingerbread, mulled wine, and traditional Bavarian sausages. It is a beautiful event that encapsulates the essence of the festive season.

Nuremberg Sausage Market

Hosted annually in Nuremberg, this festival features tastings, cooking demos, and cultural entertainment.

It's an excellent opportunity to try different types of Nuremberg sausages and learn about their history.

Bamberg Beer Week

This festival celebrates the city's diverse beer choices, including its signature Rauchbier. Visitors can tour local breweries, partake in tastings, and attend beer-themed events and entertainment.

Bavarian cuisine is a delightful tour through the region's culinary traditions, providing a diverse range of flavors and experiences. From meaty sausages and savory pig meals to sweet pastries and world-renowned beers, Bavaria's culinary scene caters to all tastes. By discovering its diverse culinary choices and embracing the local dining culture, visitors can completely immerse themselves in Bavaria's gastronomic legacy. Whether you're enjoying a lunch in a pleasant beer garden or indulging in a gourmet feast, Bavaria's culinary delights promise an amazing experience.

CHAPTER FOUR

Top Attractions and Activities in Bavaria

Bavaria is a region rich in cultural history, beautiful landscapes, and historical landmarks, with numerous attractions and activities for visitors. From fairy-tale castles and quaint medieval villages to spectacular natural wonders and bustling cultural festivals, Bavaria offers a unique experience for each visitor.

This chapter looks at the major attractions and activities that make Bavaria a must-see trip. Here are some of the top attractions in Bavaria:

The Bavarian Alps

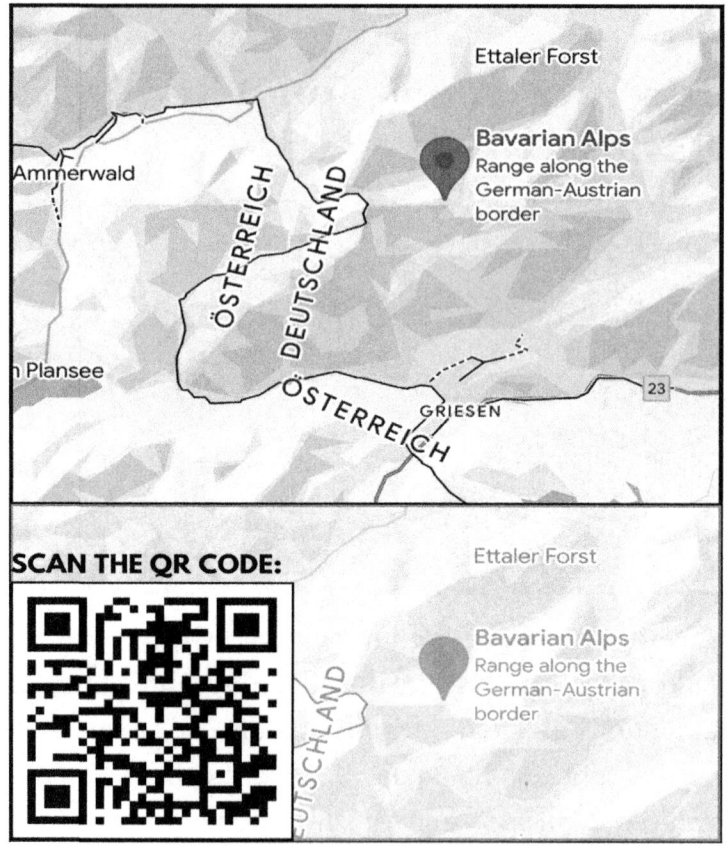

The Bavarian Alps, located in southern Germany near the Austrian border, offer a stunning landscape of rugged mountains, serene lakes, and charming alpine villages. Stretching across Bavaria, these peaks are part of the larger Alpine range and are a haven for outdoor enthusiasts, featuring world-class hiking, skiing, and mountaineering opportunities. Notable areas include Garmisch-Partenkirchen, home to Germany's highest peak, Zugspitze, and Berchtesgaden National Park. Rich in history and culture, the region also boasts fairy-tale castles like Neuschwanstein and traditional Bavarian customs, making it a popular year-round destination for nature lovers and travelers.

Munich: The Bavarian Capital

Munich, located in the southern part of Germany is the capital of Bavaria. It is a radiant city that flawlessly blends history and modernity. Known for its cultural richness, architectural beauty, and dynamic atmosphere, Munich has a wide range of attractions and activities to suit all interests.

The following are popular attractions in Munich:

Marienplatz and the Glockenspiel

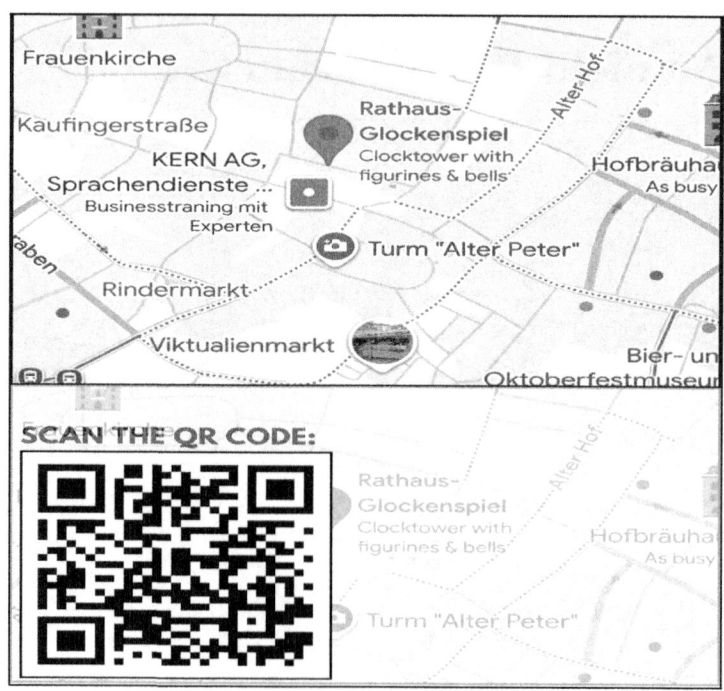

Munich's heart, Marienplatz, is a lively area surrounded by ancient buildings and colorful shops. The area is home to the Neues Rathaus (New Town Hall), featuring the famed Glockenspiel, which performs a lovely clockwork show several times a day. Visitors can enjoy the bustling environment, explore the adjacent streets, and explore the stunning architecture.

Nymphenburg Palace

Located in the western part of Munich, Nymphenburg Palace, a spectacular baroque house, is one of Munich's most visited attractions. The palace complex features beautifully designed grounds, exquisite interiors, and diverse museums displaying royal artifacts. A stroll around the enormous parkland offers a look into Bavaria's royal past.

English Garden

Located in Munich, the English Garden is one of the world's largest urban parks, providing a serene escape from the city's hustle and bustle. Visitors can take leisurely walks, picnics, or paddle boating on the park's tranquil lake. The park also features traditional beer gardens where guests can unwind with a refreshing drink.

Neuschwanstein Castle

Neuschwanstein Castle is an iconic symbol of Bavaria and one of the world's most visited castles. The castle, perched on a mountaintop near the town of Füssen, captivates visitors with its fairy-tale architecture and stunning alpine environment. Neuschwanstein's whimsical style, influenced by medieval stories, served as the inspiration for Disney's Sleeping Beauty Castle. It was built by King Ludwig II. Guided tours provide information about the castle's history and the king's eccentric life.

Nuremberg: A Medieval Gem

Nuremberg is a city steeped in history, with its well-preserved medieval architecture and diverse cultural legacy. It has a variety of attractions that reflect its historic significance and active current. The following are popular attractions in Nuremberg:

Nuremberg Castle

Located at the northern edge of Alstadt, Nuremberg Castle is a majestic fortress that dominates the city skyline. Visitors can visit the castle's towers, courtyards, and museum, which features exhibits on the city's history. The castle offers a panoramic perspective of Nuremberg's picturesque Old Town.

Documentation Center, Nazi Party Rally Grounds

Located in the southeast part of Nuremberg, this museum, situated at the former Nazi Party rally grounds, offers a sobering insight into the city's role during the Third Reich. The Documentation Center offers comprehensive exhibitions on the history of Nazi propaganda and the regime's impact, providing significant lessons for future generations.

Nuremberg Christmas Market

Located in the heart of Nuremberg's old town, the Nuremberg Christmas Market, also known as Christkindlesmarkt, is one of the world's oldest and famous Christmas marketplaces. The market, located in the city's main plaza, features lavishly adorned kiosks selling homemade goods, festive meals, and traditional Glühwein (mulled wine). The market's lovely atmosphere and cultural events make it a standout during the holiday season.

Regensburg: A UNESCO World Heritage Site

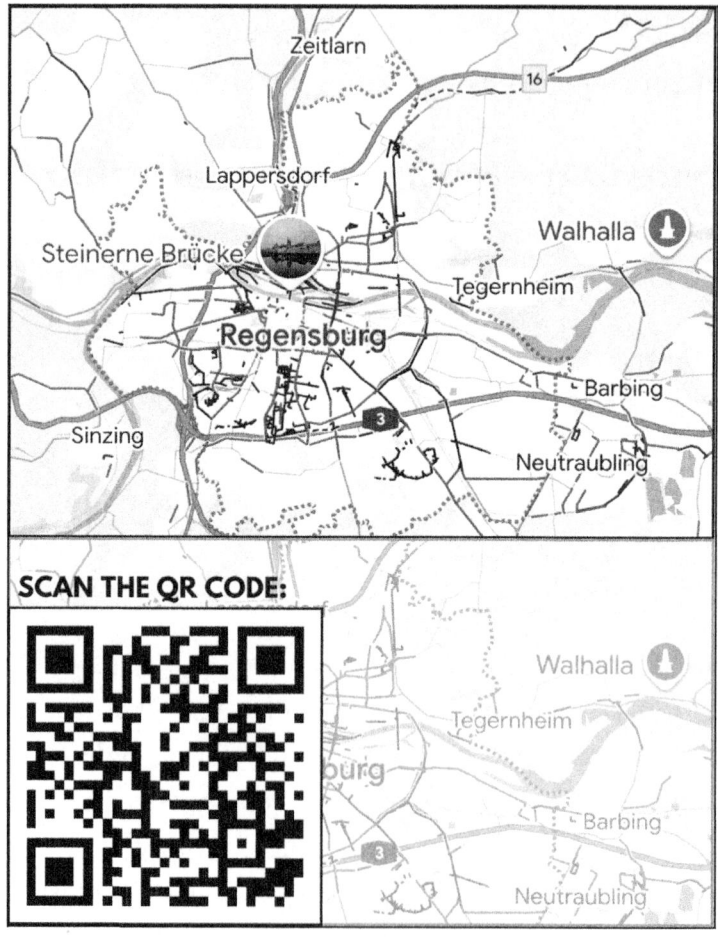

Regensburg, located on the Danube River, is a city known for its well-preserved medieval architecture and extensive history. Its Old Town is a UNESCO World Heritage Site with a variety of attractions for history buffs.

The following are popular attractions in Regensburg:

Old Stone Bridge

Located in the city of Regensburg, the Old Stone Bridge, a spectacular technical marvel from the 12th century, connects the old town to the Stadtamhof neighborhood. Visitors can walk across the bridge to experience breathtaking views of the city and the river, all while learning about its historical significance as a vital trading route.

Regensburg Cathedral

Located in the city of Regensburg, Regensburg Cathedral, also known as St. Peter's Cathedral, is an outstanding example of Gothic architecture. Its towering twin spires dominate the city skyline, and its opulent interior features stunning stained glass windows and elaborate sculptures. The Regensburger Domspatzen, the cathedral's renowned boys' choir, gives frequent performances and provides a lovely musical experience.

Bamberg: The City of Seven Hills

Bamberg is a picturesque town perched on seven hills, each crowned by a stunning church. Its Old

Town is a UNESCO World Heritage Site, known for its medieval and baroque architecture, as well as its thriving beer scene. The following are popular attractions in Regensburg:

Bamberg Cathedral

Located on the Domberg, in the heart of Bamberg's old town, Bamberg Cathedral is a stunning specimen of Romanesque architecture that houses the famous Bamberg Horseman monument. Visitors can discover the cathedral's rich history while admiring its spectacular sculptures and artworks.

Altes Rathaus (The Old Town Hall)

The Altes Rathaus is an architectural masterpiece located on an island in the midst of the Regnitz River. Its distinctive setting and vibrant frescoes make it one of Bamberg's most photographed monuments. Visitors can learn about the building's history and enjoy views of the surrounding area from the bridges.

Berchtesgaden

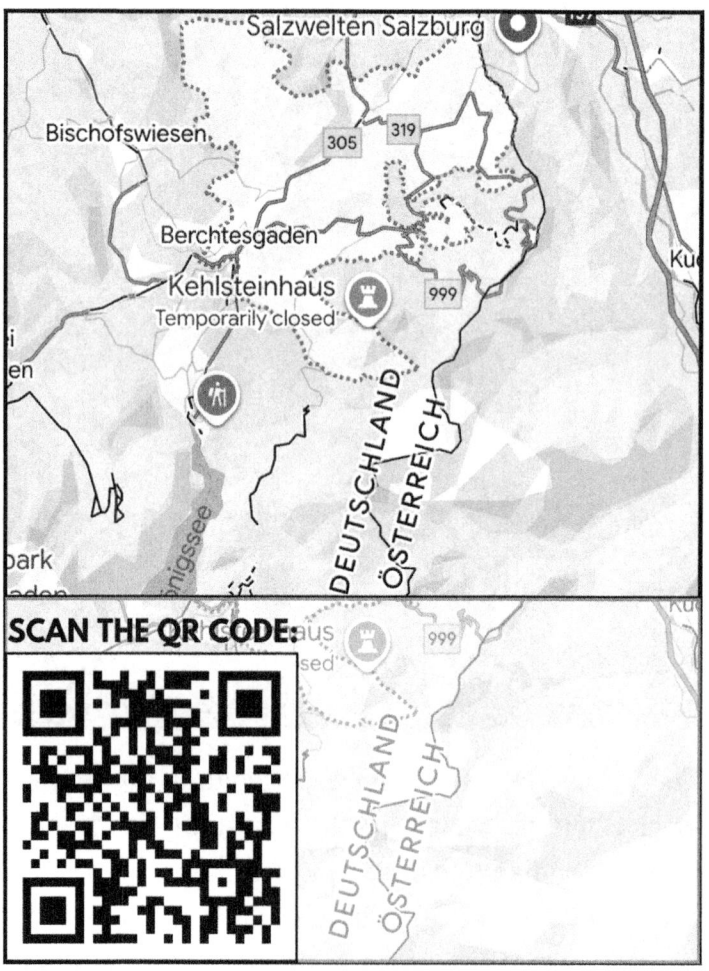

Berchtesgaden is a lovely town in the Bavarian Alps, close to the Austrian border. The town is renowned for its breathtaking natural beauty and is surrounded by magnificent mountain scenery, including the landmark Watzmann peak. Berchtesgaden is also home to the picturesque Königssee Lake and the historic Berghof, Adolf Hitler's former house. Today, it serves as the entry to Berchtesgaden National Park, where tourists can enjoy a variety of outdoor activities, rich history, and traditional Bavarian culture.

The following are popular attractions in Berchtesgaden:

Berchtesgaden National Park

Berchtesgaden National Park, located in the Bavarian Alps, is a natural wilderness area with breathtaking scenery and a variety of outdoor activities. The park's craggy mountains, lush woods, and crystal-clear lakes make it an ideal destination for nature enthusiasts and adventurers.

Eagle's Nest

The Eagle's Nest, built on a mountain top overlooking Berchtesgaden, served as Adolf Hitler's refuge during World War II. Today, it functions as a restaurant and historical landmark, with spectacular panoramic views of the surrounding Alps. The Eagle's Nest is accessible via a picturesque bus trip and an elevator.

The Romantic Road

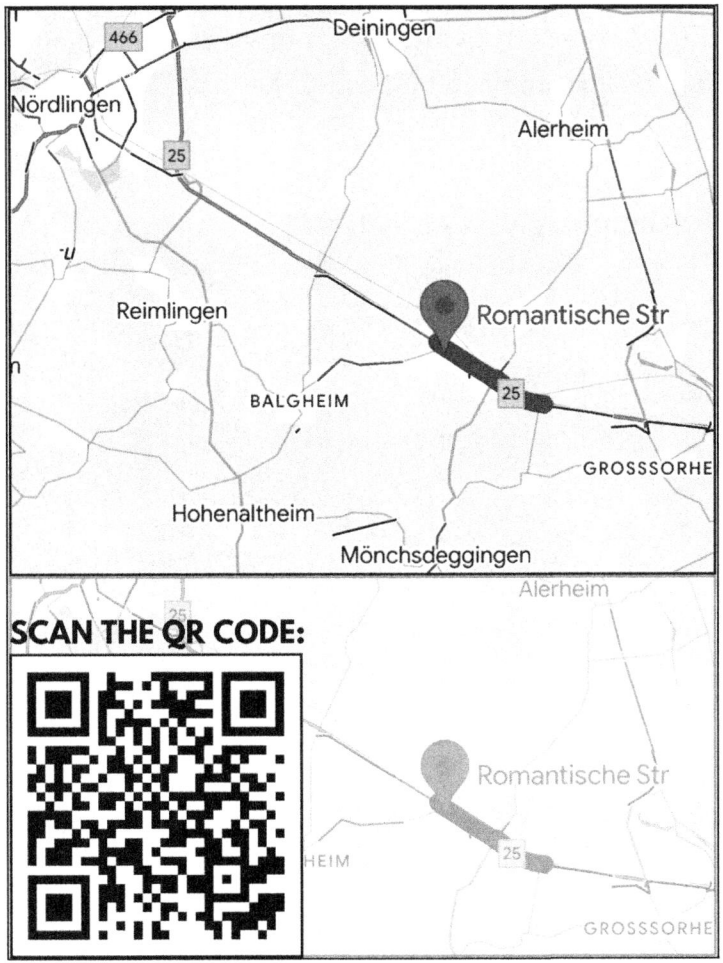

Located in southern Germany, the Romantic Road is a scenic path that connects Bavaria's stunning countryside with lovely towns and historic attractions. It is one of Germany's most popular tourist routes, providing a glimpse into the region's rich history and natural beauty.

Rothenburg ob der Tauber

Located in the Franconia region of Bavaria, Rothenburg ob der Tauber is a fairytale town famed for its well-preserved medieval architecture and magical atmosphere. Visitors can wander the town's cobblestone streets, see the old town walls, and admire the panoramic views from the Town Hall tower.

Würzburg Residence

Located in the northern part of Bavaria, the Würzburg Residence is a baroque mansion and UNESCO World Heritage Site known for its breathtaking architecture and wonderfully maintained gardens. Visitors can explore the palace's opulent halls and admire artist Giovanni Battista Tiepolo's murals.

Bavarian Festivals and Cultural Events

Bavaria has a thriving calendar of festivals and cultural events that honor its rich traditions and energetic spirit. These events offer a chance to experience Bavarian culture in a festive and social setting . The following are some of Bavaria's core festivals:

Starkbierzeit (Strong Beer Festival)

Starkbierzeit, observed in March, is a traditional Bavarian event that honors strong beer. Breweries in Munich and other cities create special high-alcohol beers to commemorate the occasion, which is accompanied by live music, substantial food, and festive activities.

The Bayreuth Festival

The Bayreuth Festival is an annual event celebrating composer Richard Wagner's works. The festival, held at Bayreuth, attracts opera aficionados from all over the world to enjoy Wagner's operas performed in the ancient Festspielhaus.

Bavaria is an area of exceptional beauty and cultural richness, with a broad range of sights and activities to suit everyone's interests. Whether you're exploring the dynamic city of Munich, marveling at fairy-tale castles, or immersing yourself in the natural marvels of the Bavarian Alps, Bavaria offers a memorable experience.

CHAPTER FIVE

Sample Itineraries

Bavaria is an area with a rich weave of culture, history, and natural beauty, providing several chances for exploration and adventure. To help you make the most of your stay, this chapter provides a selection of sample itineraries adapted to different interests and travel durations. Whether you're interested in history, nature, or family activities, these itineraries will guide you through the best that Bavaria has to offer.

Three-Day Highlights Tour

This itinerary is ideal for travelers with limited time who wish to see the highlights of Bavaria's most iconic sights.

Day One: Munich

- **Morning:** Begin your day at Marienplatz, the heart of Munich. Visit Munich's iconic cathedral, Frauenkirche, after watching the famous Glockenspiel show at the New Town Hall.

- **Afternoon:** Head to the English Garden for a leisurely stroll or a paddle boat trip and enjoy lunch at the Chinese Tower beer garden.

- **Evening:** Explore Schwabing, a dynamic district noted for its bohemian ambiance and exciting nightlife. Dine at a traditional Bavarian restaurant and try the local delights.

Day Two: Neuschwanstein and Hohenschwangau Castles

- **Morning:** Depart Munich early for a day trip to Füssen, home to the fairytale Neuschwanstein Castle. Take a guided tour of the castle's lavish interiors and learn about King Ludwig II's unusual lifestyle.

- **Afternoon:** Visit the adjacent Hohenschwangau Castle, where Ludwig spent most of his boyhood. After that, enjoy a lovely walk around the Alpsee Lake.

- **Evening:** Return to Munich and enjoy a local Bavarian dinner at Hofbräuhaus, one of the city's oldest beer halls.

Day 3: Nuremberg

- **Morning:** Travel to Nuremberg to tour the beautiful Old Town. After that, visit the Nuremberg Castle and the Albrecht Dürer's House.

- **Afternoon:** Learn about Nuremberg's role during the Third Reich at the Documentation Center Nazi Party Rally Grounds and visit the Nuremberg Trials Memorial to learn about postwar justice.

- **Evening:** Take a stroll around the lovely streets of the Old Town and eat dinner at a local restaurant. Try the popular Nuremberg sausages and gingerbread.

One-Week Cultural Exploration

This itinerary goes further into Bavaria's cultural history, providing a comprehensive examination of the region's ancient cities and towns.

Day 1–2: Munich

- **Day 1:** Follow the first day's itinerary from the Three-Day Highlights Tour, but include a visit to the Residenz Museum, the former royal palace of the Bavarian rulers.

- **Day 2:** Visit the Deutsches Museum, one of the world's largest scientific and technology museums. After that, spend the afternoon exploring the trendy Glockenbachviertel neighborhood, known for its boutiques and cafés.

Day 3–4: Regensburg and Passau

- **Day 3:** Travel to Regensburg, a UNESCO World Heritage Site. Discover the Old Town, the Stone Bridge, and St. Peter's Cathedral. After that, you can enjoy lunch at a riverbank café.

- **Day 4:** Head to Passau, known as the "City of Three Rivers." Visit St. Stephen's Cathedral, which houses the world's largest cathedral organ, and tour the Veste Oberhaus castle for panoramic views.

Day 5–6: Bamberg and Würzburg

- **Day 5:** Explore Bamberg's magnificent Old Town, a UNESCO World Heritage site, visit

Bamberg Cathedral and the Alte Rathaus and enjoy a sampling at a Rauchbier brewery.

- **Day 6:** Travel to Würzburg and visit the Würzburg Residence, a baroque masterpiece. Explore the Marienberg Fortress and the Old Main Bridge, then unwind with a wine tasting at a local vineyard.

Day 7: Rothenburg ob der Tauber

- **Morning:** Arrive in Rothenburg ob der Tauber, a legendary town on the Romantic Road. After that, take a walk along the old town walls and visit the Christmas Museum.

- **Afternoon:** Enjoy lunch at a traditional Franconian restaurant and spend the afternoon visiting the town's quaint streets and boutiques.

- **Evening:** Return to Munich or continue your tour along the Romantic Road.

Family-Friendly Adventures

This itinerary is designed for families, offering a variety of fun and educational activities to keep travelers of all ages entertained.

Day 1: Munich

- **Morning:** Visit the Hellabrunn Zoo, which houses a broad collection of animals and interactive displays.

- **Afternoon:** Visit Deutsches Museum's Kinderreich (Children's Kingdom), where children can engage with hands-on science and technology exhibits.

- **Evening:** Enjoy a family dinner at the Augustiner-Keller beer garden, which offers a playground and a laid-back ambiance.

Day 2: Legoland Deutschland

- **All Day:** Spend the day at Legoland Germany in Günzburg. Explore themed locations, take exhilarating rides, and admire the exquisite

Lego creations. The park offers attractions ideal for children of all ages.

Day 3: Neuschwanstein Castle

- **Morning:** Depart for Füssen to visit Neuschwanstein Castle. Take a horse-drawn carriage ride up to the castle for a magical experience.

- **Afternoon:** Explore the local area, including the lovely village of Schwangau and the nearby Tegelberg mountain, where you can ride a cable car to see breathtaking views.

- **Evening**: Return to Munich and unwind over a casual supper at a family-friendly restaurant.

Outdoor and Nature Lovers' Itinerary

This itinerary is ideal for travelers looking to discover Bavaria's natural splendor and participate in outdoor activities.

Day 1–2: Berchtesgaden National Park

- **Day 1:** Arrive in Berchtesgaden and visit the Dokumentation Obersalzberg for historical information. In the afternoon, go on a boat tour of Lake Königssee to see the emerald waters and visit St. Bartholomew's Church.

- **Day 2:** Hike to the Eagle's Nest for stunning views of the Bavarian Alps. Spend the afternoon exploring the park's hiking paths, which range from casual strolls to challenging climbs.

Day 3–4: Garmisch-Partenkirchen

- **Day 3:** Take a trip to Garmisch-Partenkirchen and take a cable car to Germany's highest peak, the Zugspitze. Enjoy magnificent views while exploring the glacier.

- **Day 4:** Explore the Partnach Gorge, a natural beauty with small pathways and rushing water. Spend the afternoon touring the town and relaxing at a local café.

Day 5–6: Chiemsee and Herrenchiemsee Palace

- **Day 5:** Visit Lake Chiemsee, Bavaria's largest lake. Enjoy water sports like sailing or paddleboarding, or simply relax on the lakeside beaches.

- **Day 6:** Visit Herrenchiemsee Palace, King Ludwig II's duplicate of Versailles on an island in the lake. Explore the luxurious palace and its stunning gardens.

Day 7: Bavarian Forest National Park

- **All Day:** Visit the Bavarian Forest National Park, Germany's oldest national park. Explore the deep woods, hiking paths, and wildlife exhibitions. The park is a paradise for environment lovers, with chances for bird watching and nature photography.

CHAPTER SIX

Shopping and Entertainment

Bavaria is a region that seamlessly integrates tradition and modernity, offering a thriving shopping and entertainment scene that caters to a diverse spectrum of tastes and interests. With bustling city centers full of high-end boutiques and department stores, as well as attractive markets and traditional craft shops, Bavaria is a shopper's dream. Meanwhile, its rich cultural legacy offers a wide range of entertainment alternatives, ranging from classical music and theater to modern nightlife and seasonal festivals. This chapter explores the top retail and entertainment options in Bavaria, providing insights into what makes each experience distinct.

Shopping in Bavaria

Whether you want luxury items, traditional crafts, or unique mementos, Bavaria has something for everyone. Here's a guide to some of the top places to shop in the area:

Munich: The Shopping Hub

Munich, the capital of Bavaria, is a popular shopping destination with something for everyone. The city offers a mix of luxury boutiques, department stores, and traditional marketplaces. The following are some of the best places to shop in Munich:

Maximilianstrasse

Maximilianstrasse is Munich's most prominent shopping boulevard, famous for its luxury boutiques and high-end designer brands. Here you'll find designer labels like Chanel, Louis Vuitton, and Gucci, as well as luxury jewelry stores and art galleries. This boulevard is ideal for people who want to indulge in luxury shopping.

Kaufingerstrasse and Marienplatz

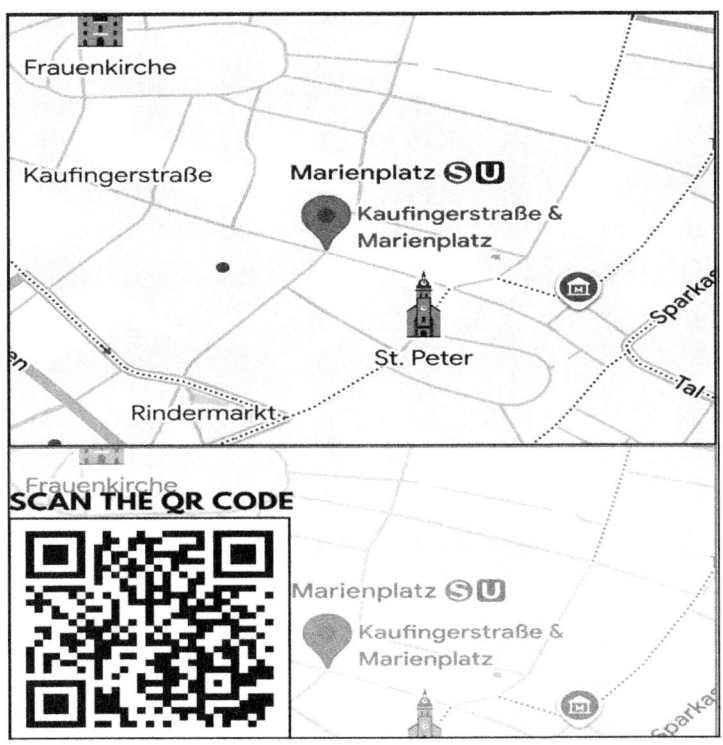

SCAN THE QR CODE

Kaufingerstrasse, one of the city's oldest streets, connects Marienplatz to Karlsplatz and offers more conventional shopping options. This pedestrian zone is lined with well-known department stores like Galeria Kaufhof, worldwide brands like H&M, Zara, and a variety of specialty businesses. Marienplatz, the city's principal square, also hosts seasonal markets, including the popular Christmas market.

Nuremberg: Traditional Crafts and Markets

Nuremberg is well-known for its traditional craftsmanship and medieval marketplaces, making it an ideal destination for people looking for unique souvenirs and handmade items. Below is one of the best places to shop in Nuremberg:

Handwerkerhof

Located near the city's major train station, Handwerkerhof is a lovely medieval-style courtyard where traditional craftspeople sell their items. Handcrafted objects include pottery, jewelry, leather goods, and toys. The atmosphere is reminiscent of a bygone period, making shopping an enjoyable experience.

Regensburg: Historical Shopping Streets

Regensburg, a UNESCO World Heritage site, provides a distinctive shopping experience with its well-preserved medieval alleyways and lovely boutiques. Below is one of the best places to shop in Nuremberg:

Haidplatz

Haidplatz is a scenic plaza surrounded by ancient buildings, with a variety of specialty stores and cafés. This area is ideal for casual shopping, with a mix of traditional Bavarian goods and modern products. Don't pass up the opportunity to visit local confectioneries and bakeries for some delectable treats.

Ingolstadt Village: Outlet Shopping

Ingolstadt Village, located just outside of Munich, is a luxury outlet shopping destination that provides discounts on high-end brands. Over 110 boutiques can be found in the open-air shopping village, featuring international brands like Prada, Burberry, and Versace. It's an excellent choice for fashion enthusiasts looking for high-quality items at discounted prices.

Bamberg: Antiques and Local Specialties

Bamberg's picturesque Old Town and rich history make it a one-of-a-kind shopping destination for antiques and local specialties. Below is one of the best places to shop in Bamberg:

Grüner Markt

Grüner Markt is Bamberg's central marketplace, offering a wide range of local products such as fresh fruit, cheeses, and baked goods. The market also has several specialty shops that serve Bamberg's famous Rauchbier (smoked beer) and other regional specialties.

Antiques and Artisans

Bamberg is well-known for its antique shops and artisan businesses, particularly in the Sandstrasse area. Visitors can look through a collection of antiques, including furniture, paintings, and decorative items, as well as artisan goods like pottery and fabrics.

Entertainment in Bavaria

Bavaria has a diverse range of entertainment options, from classical music and theater to colorful festivals and sophisticated nightlife. The region's cultural heritage ensures that there is something to suit every taste. The following are some of the top festivals and entertainment options in Bavaria:

Classical Music and Opera

Bavaria has a strong classical music legacy, with many well-known composers having lived and worked there. For classical music enthusiasts, there are several options to see world-class concerts. Below is a top classical music and opera establishment in Bavaria:

Munich Philharmonic and the Bavarian State Opera

The Munich Philharmonic and Bavarian State Opera are among Germany's most famous institutions. The Philharmonic presents a diverse spectrum of symphonic concerts, while the State Opera is well-known for its presentations of classical operas and ballets. Both are housed in beautiful historic venues, offering a refined night out for music lovers.

Theater and Performing Arts

Bavaria's thriving theatrical scene features a wide spectrum of performances, including classical plays, current productions, and experimental theater. The following are top theatrical establishments in Bavaria:

Residenztheater, Munich

The Residenztheater in Munich is one of Bavaria's major drama and performing arts theaters. The theater showcases a diverse range of productions, including traditional German plays, international works, and avant-garde performances. The historic structure enhances the experience, providing an insight into Bavaria's cultural legacy.

Nuremberg State Theater

The Nuremberg State Theatre (Staatstheater Nürnberg) is a well-known cultural institution in the heart of Nuremberg, Germany. It stages a wide variety of productions, including opera, ballet, drama, and concerts. The theater, located in a historic structure with spectacular architecture, is well-known for its rich tradition and high-quality plays. It acts as a cultural focus for the city, attracting both locals and visitors with its colorful programming and creative excellence.

Nightlife and Modern Entertainment

Bavaria's cities have an active nightlife culture, with a mix of classic beer halls, trendy bars, and exciting clubs. Below is a closer look at Bavaria's nightlife and modern entertainment scene:

Munich's Nightlife

Munich's nightlife is diverse and colorful, appealing to all preferences. The city is well-known for its beer halls, such as Hofbräuhaus and Augustiner-Keller, where visitors can enjoy a lively environment and traditional Bavarian music. For a more modern experience, visit the Glockenbachviertel or Schwabing districts, where you'll find trendy bars, cocktail lounges, and nightclubs.

Nuremberg's Red Bull District

Nuremberg's Red Bull District is the city's leading nightlife destination, with a diverse selection of bars, clubs, and live music venues. The district is especially popular among young residents and visitors looking for a night of dancing and entertainment.

CHAPTER SEVEN

Outdoor and Adventure Activities

Bavaria is a haven for outdoor enthusiasts, with a wide range of activities that take full advantage of the spectacular natural settings. From the towering peaks of the Bavarian Alps to the tranquil lakes and deep forests, Bavaria's diverse environment provides the ideal setting for adventure. Whether you are a seasoned mountaineer, a casual hiker, or someone seeking a quiet retreat in nature, Bavaria has something for you. This chapter delves into the top outdoor and adventure activities in the region, highlighting the best locations for each.

Hiking and Walking Trails

Bavaria is crisscrossed with a vast network of hiking and walking routes suitable for all levels of experience. The region's diverse landscapes, ranging from mild rolling hills to demanding mountain routes, make it an ideal hiking destination. Below are some of the top hiking and walking trails in Bavaria:

The Bavarian Forest National Park

Located on the southeastern part of Germany, near the border with the Czech Republic, the Bavarian

Forest National Park, Germany's first national park, is ideal for nature enthusiasts and hikers. The park is recognized for its lush forests, tranquil lakes, and diverse wildlife. The Lusen Mountain hike is one of the park's highlights, offering a challenging ascent through old forests to a rocky summit with spectacular views. The Baumwipfelpfad, or tree-top walk, offers a unique perspective by allowing tourists to walk among the treetops and take in the breathtaking views of the forest canopy.

The Altmühltal Valley Nature Park

Located in the central part of Bavaria, primarily along the Altmühl River, the Altmühltal Nature Park has a number of picturesque walking and cycling routes for those seeking easier terrain, The

Altmühltal Panorama Trail is very popular, winding through undulating hills, limestone cliffs, and picturesque villages. The park also contains various historical sites, including Roman ruins and medieval castles, making it an ideal destination for people looking to combine outdoor sports with cultural exploration.

Skiing and Snowboarding

Bavaria's snow-capped mountains offer some of the best skiing and snowboarding opportunities in Germany. The region's ski resorts accommodate all skill levels, from beginner slopes to challenging off-piste lines. The following are some of the top skiing and snowboarding spots in Bavaria:

Garmisch-Partenkirchen

Located in southern Germany, near the border of Austria, Garmisch-Partenkirchen is Bavaria's most famous ski resort, with world-class amenities and breathtaking mountain scenery. The resort is home to Germany's tallest peak, the Zugspitze, which has a range of slopes suited for skiers and snowboarders of all skill levels. The resort also holds international tournaments, such as the FIS Alpine Ski World Cup, making it a popular destination for winter sports fans.

Oberstdorf

Oberstdorf, located in the Allgäu Alps, is another popular ski destination in Bavaria. The resort is renowned for its extensive network of slopes, especially the Nebelhorn, which has Germany's longest downhill run. Oberstdorf is also famous for its ski jumping facilities, which host the annual Four Hills Tournament. In addition to skiing and snowboarding, visitors can go snowshoeing, ice skating, or tobogganing.

Berchtesgaden

Berchtesgaden is a picturesque ski resort with a more casual and family-oriented vibe. The resort's Jennerbahn region provides a range of slopes for both beginners and intermediate skiers, as well as breathtaking views of the surrounding Alps. Berchtesgaden is also famous for its outstanding cross-country skiing tracks that snake through the magnificent mountain scenery.

Cycling and Mountain Biking

Bavaria is a cyclist's dream, with a well-kept network of cycling paths and mountain biking trails that pass through some of the region's most scenic landscapes. The following are some of the top mountain biking and cycling spots in Bavaria:

Lake Chiemsee

Located on the southeastern part of Germany, Lake Chiemsee, known as the "Bavarian Sea," is famous for cyclists. The Chiemsee Circular Route is a 60-kilometer path that circles the lake, providing breathtaking views of both the water and the surrounding mountains. Cyclists can also take a break to see the lake's islands, such as Herreninsel, home to the stunning Herrenchiemsee Palace.

The Bavarian Alps

For mountain bikers, the Bavarian Alps provide tough tracks with thrilling descents and breathtaking views. The trails around Garmisch-Partenkirchen and Oberstdorf are particularly popular, with routes suitable for all skill levels. The paths frequently travel through alpine meadows, woodlands, and high-altitude terrain, providing a thrilling experience for adventurers.

Water Sports

Bavaria's lakes and rivers offer ample opportunities for water sports, including sailing, windsurfing, kayaking, and canoeing. The following are some of the top spots for water sports in Bavaria:

Lake Starnberg

Lake Starnberg, just south of Munich, is a popular spot for sailing and windsurfing. The lake's tranquil waters and picturesque surroundings make it ideal for a day on the water. Several marinas around the lake provide boat rentals and sailing courses, making it accessible to both new and experienced sailors.

Lake Königssee

Situated within the Berchtesgaden Land district, Lake Königssee, with its crystal-clear waters and dramatic mountain backdrop, is one of Bavaria's most beautiful lakes. The lake is ideal for kayaking and canoeing, allowing guests to explore the tranquil waters at their own speed. Boat cruises are also offered, providing a more relaxed way to enjoy the breathtaking scenery.

Isar River

Located in southern Germany, the Isar River, which flows through Munich and the Bavarian Alps, is a famous rafting and kayaking destination. The river's upper stretches provide thrilling rapids for more experienced paddlers, while the sections closer to Munich are milder and suited for beginners. The river also runs through some of Bavaria's most attractive landscapes, creating a picturesque backdrop for water-based adventures.

Climbing and Mountaineering

Bavaria's rough mountains provide good chances for climbing and mountaineering, with routes suitable for both novice and experienced climbers. The following are some of the top climbing and mountaineering spots in Bavaria:

Zugspitze

Located in the Bavarian Alps, the Zugspitze, Germany's highest mountain, is a popular destination for mountaineers. Several routes lead to the peak, ranging from challenging hikes to tricky climbs. The most famous route is the Höllental Valley climb, which combines hiking, climbing, and glacier crossings. For those seeking a less rigorous experience, a cable car can transport visitors close to the summit, allowing them to enjoy panoramic views without having to climb.

Franconian Switzerland

Franconian Switzerland, located in northern Bavaria, is a well-known climbing location with hundreds of routes appropriate for all skill levels. The region's limestone cliffs and rock formations offer a wide variety of climbing opportunities, from sport climbing to traditional routes. The area is also famous for its lovely villages and castles, making it an ideal location for climbers looking to combine adventure with cultural exploration.

Paragliding and Hang Gliding

Bavaria's spectacular landscapes and suitable wind conditions make it an ideal location for paragliding and hang gliding. Several locations throughout the region provide opportunities for both new and experienced pilots to take to the skies. The following are some of the top paragliding and hang gliding spots in Bavaria:

Tegelberg

Tegelberg, near Füssen, is one of Bavaria's best paragliding and hang gliding spots. The mountain's slopes make for great launching conditions, and the views of Neuschwanstein Castle and the surrounding Alps are simply stunning. Tandem flights are available for individuals who want to experience the excitement of paragliding without prior experience.

Brauneck

Brauneck, near the town of Lenggries, is another renowned paragliding spot. The mountain has various launch sites, and the surrounding environment of the Isar Valley and Karwendel Mountains provides stunning aerial views. Schools in the vicinity provide lessons and tandem flights, making it accessible for beginners.

Bavaria's diverse landscapes offer a wide range of outdoor and adventure activities to suit all interests and skill levels. Whether you're hiking through alpine meadows, skiing down snow-covered slopes, cycling along scenic roads, or soaring over the Alps, Bavaria has unlimited possibilities for exploration and adventure. The region's natural beauty, along with its rich cultural legacy, ensures that every outdoor activity is an unforgettable experience.

CHAPTER EIGHT

Local Insights and Tips

Bavaria, with its rich cultural heritage, stunning scenery, and warm hospitality, provides travelers with an immersive experience. To make the most of your vacation, it's important to be aware of local customs, traditions, and helpful tips that can enhance your journey. This chapter provides essential insights and suggestions to help you navigate Bavarian culture and make the most of your stay.

Understanding Bavarian Culture

Bavaria has a strong cultural identity, influenced by centuries of history, religion, and custom. Understanding and respecting these cultural subtleties can significantly improve your trip experience. The following are core aspects of Bavarian Culture:

Bavarian Pride

Bavarians are noted for their strong regional pride, typically identifying as Bavarian first, and German second. This pride is demonstrated by the preservation of local traditions, dialects, and customs. Accentuate this regional identity by participating in local events, learning a few Bavarian words, and demonstrating your admiration for the region's distinct culture.

Traditional Clothing

During festivals and special events, Bavarians are frequently dressed in traditional Tracht. Men wear Lederhosen (leather shorts) with a checkered shirt, while women wear Dirndls (colorful gowns with fitting bodices and voluminous skirts). If you intend to attend an event like Oktoberfest or a local festival, consider renting or purchasing Tracht to fully immerse yourself in the atmosphere.

Religion and Holidays

Bavaria is largely Catholic, and religion is a significant part of everyday life. Many Bavarian villages have a church at their center, and religious holidays are celebrated with solemnity. Be aware that some shops and businesses may be closed on Sundays and religious holidays, such as Easter, Christmas, and Corpus Christi. Additionally, if you visit a church or religious site, dress modestly and respect local customs.

Practical Travel Tips

Traveling in Bavaria can be a straightforward and delightful experience with proper planning and awareness of local practices. Below is a closer look at this aspect:

Public Transportation

Bavaria has an efficient and comprehensive public transportation network, which includes trains, buses, and trams. The Deutsche Bahn (DB) railway system connects large cities and towns, while smaller buses and trams provide easy access within cities. Consider obtaining a Bayern-Ticket, which offers unlimited travel on regional trains and public transportation throughout Bavaria for a day, making it an affordable option for visiting various destinations.

Dinner Etiquette

Dining in Bavaria is often a casual and convivial occasion, however there are a few customs to be aware of:

- **Tipping:** It is customary to round up the bill and leave a 5-10% tip for good service. When paying, tip the server directly.

- **Sharing Tables:** Strangers frequently share tables at beer gardens and restaurants. Before you join, simply ask if a seat is still available with the phrase "Ist hier noch frei?"

- **Meal Times:** Lunch (Mittagessen) is traditionally the main meal of the day, served between 12:00 and 2:00 p.m. Dinner (Abendessen) is typically lighter and served early in the evening.

Responsible Travel

Bavaria's natural beauty and cultural history are best enjoyed with a commitment to responsible and sustainable travel practices. The following are some important aspects of practicing responsible travel in Bavaria:

Environmental Responsibility

Bavarians take pride in their natural surroundings, and visitors are encouraged to do the same. Here are some tips to reducing your environmental impact:

- **Recycle:** Bavaria has an extensive recycling system, so be sure to properly sort your trash using the appropriate bins.

- **Use Public Transport:** Reduce your carbon footprint by opting for public transit or cycling instead of driving.

- **Respect Nature**: Stick to marked pathways in national parks and nature reserves and avoid disturbing wildlife.

Supporting Local Communities

Supporting local businesses and artisans not only enhances your trip experience, but also contributes to the local economy. Consider lodging at family-run guesthouses, dining at locally owned restaurants, and buying gifts from local artisans. This approach ensures that your visit has a beneficial impact on the communities you come across.

Cultural Sensitivity

Respecting local customs and traditions is essential for a great travel experience. When visiting religious places, adhere to local clothing requirements, be mindful of noise levels in residential areas, and always seek permission before taking photos of people. Engaging with locals in a courteous and open-minded manner can help you understand Bavarian culture and make unforgettable memories.

Bavaria is a destination unlike any other, with its rich culture, friendly locals, and breathtaking landscapes. Understanding and embracing local customs, preparing for practical travel scenarios, and committing to responsible tourism will ensure that your trip to Bavaria is not only fun but also respectful of the region's legacy and environment. The above insights and tips will help you navigate Bavarian life with ease, allowing you to fully immerse yourself in all that this beautiful region has to offer.

CHAPTER NINE

Resources and Contacts

Traveling through Bavaria can be a rewarding and seamless experience if you have the correct resources and contacts. Whether you're seeking tourist information, emergency assistance, or handy apps, having dependable resources at your disposal will make your journey easier. This chapter provides a comprehensive list of essential contacts and resources to help you prepare for any problem that may arise during your Bavarian adventure or vacation.

Tourist Information Centers

Tourist information centers are useful resources for visitors, offering maps, brochures, and professional advice on local attractions, lodgings, and events. Bavaria has a well-developed network of these centers, which are often positioned in city centers, near major sights, and at transit hubs. The following are some of the major tourist information centers in Bavaria:

Munich Tourist Information

- **Location:** Marienplatz, München.
- **Contact**: +49 89 233 96500.
- **Website:** www.muenchen.de
- **Services:** The Munich Tourist Information center offers thorough information on city tours, cultural events, transportation, and lodgings. They also provide multilingual support and can help you book tickets and arrange guided tours.

Nuremberg Tourist Information

- **Location:** Hauptmarkt 18, Nuremberg. **Contact:** +49 911 23360.
- **Website:** www.tourismus.nuernberg.de
- **Services:** This center, located in the heart of Nuremberg's Old Town, provides maps, brochures, and information on exploring the city's historic landmarks. The staff can assist you with reservations for city tours, activities, and accommodations.

Regensburg Tourist Information

- **Location:** Rathausplatz 4, Regensburg.
- **Contact:** +49 941 5074410.
- **Website:** www.regensburg.de/tourismus
- **Services:** This center provides information on Regensburg's UNESCO World Heritage sites, guided excursions, and local activities. Visitors can also buy souvenirs and local products at the center.

Bavarian Alps Tourist Information

- **Location:** A variety of locations across the Bavarian Alps including Garmisch-Partenkirchen, Füssen and Berchtesgaden.
- **Contact Details:** Varies by location.
- **Website: :** https://bavaria.travel/
- **Services:** These centers offer information on outdoor activities, hiking trails, ski resorts, and lodgings in the Bavarian Alps. They also provide weather updates and safety tips for mountain activities.

Emergency Contacts

Being prepared for emergencies is essential when traveling. Fortunately, Bavaria's emergency response system is well-organized, with services available in multiple languages.

Emergency Numbers

- **Police:** 110.
- **Fire Department:** 112.
- **Ambulance/Medical Emergencies:** 112.

The above numbers are free to call from any phone, and operators frequently provide assistance in English. Bavaria's emergency services are highly efficient, with quick response times.

Medical Assistance

Bavaria has an extensive healthcare system, with a wide range of hospitals and clinics across the region. In the event of a medical emergency, you can visit the local hospital emergency department (Notaufnahme) or dial 112 to request an ambulance.

For non-emergency medical issues, you can find pharmacies (Apotheken) in most cities and towns. Many pharmacies display a green cross outside and provide over-the-counter medications as well as guidance. For after-hours pharmaceutical services, look for signage indicating the nearest open pharmacy (Notdienst).

Lost and Found

If you lose something while traveling, contact the local police station or the lost and found office (Fundbüro) in the city where you misplaced the item. Many cities also offer online lost and found services, allowing you to report lost things and check if they have been found.

Helpful Apps and Websites

Modern technology can significantly improve your travel experience by providing quick access to maps, transportation schedules, language translation, and other resources. Here are some useful applications and websites to download before you embark on your journey to Bavaria.

Deutsche Bahn App

- **Purpose:** Public transportation.
- **Website:** www.bahn.com
- **Features:** The Deutsche Bahn app provides real-time train timetables,

- ticket booking, and route planning across Germany, including Bavaria. It is a must-have for anyone using the extensive train network.

Bayern Info

- **Purpose:** Travel planning and travel updates.
- **Website:** www.bayerninfo.de
- **Features:** Bayern Info provides real-time traffic updates, public transit information, and route planning for drivers, cyclists, and public transport users. The app also contains information on road conditions and travel times.

Google Maps

- **Purpose:** Navigation and local discovery.
- **Website:** www.google.com/maps
- **Features:** Google Maps is important for navigating Bavaria's cities and countryside. It

offers directions for driving, walking, cycling, and public transportation, as well as information on nearby sights, restaurants, and services.

TripAdvisor

- **Purpose:** Reviews of restaurants, hotels, and activity suggestions.
- **Website:** www.tripadvisor.com
- **Features:** TripAdvisor provides reviews and recommendations for hotels, restaurants, and attractions in Bavaria. It's a great website for discovering the best local spots and planning activities.

Duolingo

- **Purpose**: Language learning.
- **Website:** www.duolingo.com
- **Features:** Duolingo is a popular language study software that can help you pick up

basic German phrases before and during your trip. It's a fun and interactive method to develop your language skills and socialize with locals.

Travel Insurance

Travel insurance is highly recommended for any trip to Bavaria. It covers medical crises, vacation cancellations, lost luggage, and other unforeseen circumstances. Ensure that your travel insurance policy covers medical expenses in Germany, and carry a copy of your policy and emergency contact information with you at all times.

Consulates and Embassies

In the event of a legal issue, a missing passport, or any emergency, your country's consulate or embassy can provide essential assistance. Major cities in Bavaria, such as Munich, have several foreign consulates. The following are some of the major consulates in Bavaria:

U.S. Consulate General Munich

- **Location**: Königinstrasse 5, 80539 Munich.
- **Contact:** +49 89 2888 0.
- **Website:** https://de.usembassy.gov/
- **Services:** The US Consulate General in Munich provides passport services, emergency assistance, and legal help to US citizens.

British Consulate General Munich

- **Location:** Möhlstrasse 5, 81675 Munich.
- **Contact:** +49 89 211 090.
- **Website:** https://www.gov.uk/world/organisations/british-consulate-general-munich/office/british-consulate-general-munich
- **Services:** The British Consulate General in Munich provides passport renewal services,

emergency assistance, and consular services to British nationals.

Canadian Consulate Munich

- **Location:** Tal 29, 80331 Munich.
- **Contact:** +49 89 2199 570.
- **Website:**
  https://www.international.gc.ca/country-pays/germany-allemagne/munich.aspx?lang=eng
- **Services:** The Canadian Consulate offers emergency assistance, consular services, and legal advice to Canadian citizens.

BONUS SECTION

Hidden Gems in Bavaria

Bavaria is well-known for its renowned attractions like Neuschwanstein Castle and Oktoberfest, but the region also has a plethora of lesser-known gems that provide unique and authentic experiences away from the typical tourist routes. Exploring these hidden gems allows visitors to see a quieter, more intimate side of Bavaria, where tradition, natural beauty, and history coexist in exquisite harmony.

Blautopf, Blaubeuren

The Blautopf, located in the village of Blaubeuren, in the state of Baden-Württemberg, Germany, is a breathtaking natural spring with a vivid blue color that appears surreal. The spring is entrenched in local legend and has inspired numerous myths, adding to its allure. The surrounding area features attractive walking trails through lush forests and along the river, making it an ideal day trip for nature lovers.

Oberammergau

Oberammergau is a little village in the Bavarian Alps known for its elaborate Lüftlmalerei (traditional frescoes) that adorn the facades of its buildings. The village is also known for its Passion Play, performed every ten years by local residents. Beyond its cultural significance, Oberammergau is bordered by stunning alpine scenery that provides good hiking opportunities.

Weltenburg Abbey

Weltenburg Abbey, located along the Danube River near Kelheim, is home to the world's oldest monastic brewery, which dates back to 1050. The abbey itself is a gem of Baroque architecture, with a magnificently designed cathedral and a peaceful riverfront location. Visitors can take a boat ride down the Danube Gorge before sampling the abbey's famous dark beer, brewed by the monks.

Passau: The Three Rivers City

Tucked away on Bavaria's southeastern border, Passau is a unique and under-visited city where the Danube, Inn, and Ilz rivers converge. The town's Italianate architecture, a result of being rebuilt by Italian architects after a devastating fire in the 17th century, sets it apart from other German cities. Don't miss the "St. Stephen's Cathedral", home to the largest pipe organ in Europe. Passau's quaint old town, with its narrow, winding streets and vibrant riverside cafes, is a delightful place to explore.

Würzburg: Wine, History, and Baroque Grandeur

Often overlooked in favor of Munich or Nuremberg, Würzburg is a Baroque city known for its vineyards and architectural splendor. The "Würzburg Residence", a UNESCO World Heritage Site, is an extravagant palace with stunning frescoes and beautiful gardens. The city is also the gateway to the "Romantic Road", a scenic route that winds through some of Bavaria's most charming towns. Wine lovers should visit the "Alte Mainbrücke", the old bridge where locals gather to enjoy a glass of Franconian wine while taking in views of the river and the "Marienberg Fortress".

Ammersee and Andechs Monastery

While Lake Ammersee is less famous than Bavaria's other lakes, it's a peaceful retreat just a short drive from Munich. Surrounded by rolling hills and quaint villages, it's a perfect spot for sailing, swimming, or simply relaxing by the water. A short hike from the lake will take you to "Andechs Monastery", a Benedictine abbey known for its beer, which has been brewed by the monks for centuries. The abbey's beer garden offers fantastic views over the lake and the surrounding countryside.

Mittenwald: The Violin-Making Village

Nestled in the Bavarian Alps, Mittenwald is a charming village renowned for its violin-making tradition. Its colorful, frescoed buildings, known as "Lüftlmalerei", give the village a storybook feel. For centuries, Mittenwald has been a center of high-quality violin production, and visitors can learn about this craft at the "Geigenbau Museum". Surrounded by the towering "Karwendel mountains", Mittenwald is also a fantastic destination for hiking, with trails leading to stunning alpine vistas.

Tegernsee: Alpine Serenity

Lake Tegernsee, located just an hour's drive from Munich, is a peaceful alpine lake that offers an idyllic escape from the city. The surrounding mountains and crystal-clear waters make it a favorite among locals, but it remains less crowded than other Bavarian lakes. The town of Tegernsee is home to a former Benedictine abbey, now a brewery, where visitors can sample excellent Bavarian beer while enjoying lake views. Tegernsee is perfect for hiking, cycling, or simply relaxing by the water.

The Wieskirche: Pilgrimage Church in the Meadow

Hidden away in a quiet meadow near Steingaden, the Wieskirche (Church of the Wies) is a rococo masterpiece. Despite its secluded location, this UNESCO World Heritage Site is one of Bavaria's most stunning churches. The church's ornate interior is an astonishing contrast to its modest pastoral surroundings, making it a striking and serene place to visit.

Landshut: A Medieval Town Frozen in Time

Landshut, located along the Isar River, is often overlooked by tourists. Its medieval old town is one of the best-preserved in Bavaria, with colorful gothic buildings, cobblestone streets, and an impressive castle, "Burg Trausnitz", perched above the city. Every four years, the city hosts the "Landshut Wedding", a grand historical reenactment that draws locals and visitors alike.

These hidden gems offer a quieter, more intimate experience of Bavaria, allowing travelers to connect with the region's traditions, landscapes, and history without the hustle of more crowded destinations. Whether you're drawn to alpine villages, medieval towns, or natural wonders, Bavaria's secret treasures are waiting to be discovered.

Basic Vocabularies In German

Here are fifty basic German vocabulary words and phrases in different contexts that travelers can use as a guide:

Greetings and Basics

- **Hallo:** Hello.
- **Guten Morgen:** Good morning.
- **Guten Tag:** Good day.
- **Guten Abend:** Good evening.
- **Gute Nacht:** Good night.
- **Tschüss:** Goodbye.
- **Bitte:** Please.

- **Danke:** Thank you.
- **Entschuldigung:** Excuse me.
- **Ja:** Yes.
- **Nein:** No.

Directions and Navigation

- **Wo ist...?** - Where is...?
- **Links:** Left.
- **Rechts:** Right.
- **Geradeaus:** Straight ahead.
- **Bahnhof:** Train Station.
- **Flughafen:** Airport.
- **Straße:** Street.
- **Stadtzentrum:** City Center.

Dining and Food

- **Speisekarte:** Menu.
- **Wasser:** Water.
- **Bier:** Beer.

- **Rechnung:** Bill/check.
- **Kaffee:** Coffee.
- **Essen**: Food.
- **Brot:** Bread.
- **Fleisch:** Meat.
- **Fisch:** Fish.
- **Obst:** Fruit.
- **Gemüse:** Vegetables.

Accommodation

- **Hotel:** Hotel.
- **Zimmer:** Room.
- **Bett:** Bed.
- **Reservierung**: Reservation.
- **Schlüssel:** Key.

Numbers

- **Eins:** One.
- **Zwei:** Two.
- **Drei:** Three.

- **Vier:** Four.
- **Fünf:** Five.
- **Zehn:** Ten.
- **Zwanzig:** Twenty.
- **Hundert:** Hundred.
- **Tausend:** Thousand.

Common Objects

- **Buch:** Book.
- **Stuhl:** Chair.
- **Tisch:** Table.
- **Fenster:** Window.
- **Tür:** Door.

These terms and phrases will assist travelers navigate basic interactions in Bavaria, from greeting locals to getting around, and dining out.